Luz Bones

Also by Myrna Stone

In the Present Tense: Portraits of My Father
March 25, 2013, paperback, White Violet Press (a division of Kelsay Books)

The Casanova Chronicles
July 1, 2010, paperback, Etruscan Press

How Else to Love The World
October 2, 2007, paperback, Browser Books Publishing

The Art of Loss
May, 2001, paperback, Michigan State University Press

Luz Bones

MYRNA STONE

etruscan press

Etruscan Press
Wilkes University
84 West South Street
Wilkes-Barre, PA 18766
(570) 408-4546

WILKES UNIVERSITY

www.etruscanpress.org

Published 2017 by Etruscan Press
Printed in the United States of America
Design by Julianne Popovec
The text of this book is set in Calluna.

First Edition

16 17 18 19 20 5 4 3 2 1

Library of Congress Cataloging-in-Publication Data

Names: Stone, Myrna, 1944- author.
Title: Luz bones / Myrna Stone.
Description: Wilkes-Barre, PA : Etruscan Press, 2017.
Identifiers: LCCN 2016037380 | ISBN 9780997745511 (softcover)
Subjects: | BISAC: POETRY / American / General.
Classification: LCC PS3619.T66 A6 2017 | DDC 811/.6--dc23
LC record available at https://lccn.loc.gov/2016037380

Please turn to the back of this book for a list of the sustaining funders of
Etruscan Press.

This book is printed on recycled, acid-free paper.

For all those who paved the way

and for Tom

There is no birth, there is no death; there is no coming, there is no going; there is no same, there is no different; there is no permanent self, there is no annihilation. We only think there is.

—Thich Nhat Hanh, *No Death, No Fear*

Acknowledgments

I wish to thank the other members of The Greenville Poets for their consistently apt advice concerning these poems, and for their always sterling support. I couldn't have done this without them. I also wish to express my thanks to Phil Brady, Bill Schneider, Heather Taylor, and the rest of the wonderful staff at Etruscan who have made the experience of putting this book together a real pleasure.

Grateful acknowledgment is also made to the editors of the following publications in which these poems first appeared.

Barrow Street: "Lucy Bakewell Announces Her Imminent Marriage to John James Audubon in a Letter to Her Kinswoman, Miss Gifford"

Innisfree Poetry Journal: "To My Parents in the Hereafter," "Nok Thai in Mourning for Her Husband," "Nok Thai on the Thought of New Lives for Herself and Her Children," "Captain Abel Coffin on How He and His Partner, Robert Hunter, Have Managed the Twins on Tour," "I, Chang-Eng," "Nancy Yates on Her Daughters' Upcoming Double Nuptials," "I, Chang-Eng," "Aunt Grace Yates on the Brink of Change," "Dr. James Calloway, to His Protégé, on His History with the Bunker Brothers," "Sally Bunker Looks Back on Her Marriage," "Addie Bunker on Her Sister and Their Conjoined and Separate Lives," "Robert Bunker Describes the Circumstances of His Father's Death"

Mad River Review: "The Rev. Donald Cargill's Brother, James, on Following a Merchant's Path," "Elena to Her Second Husband, Niccolo, on the Failings of Her First Husband," "H. L. Describes

His Recent Near-Death Experience to the Newest Member of His Sex Addiction Therapy Group," "H. L.'s Former Wife, Mary, on His Checkered History," "Paul Novak to Attorney Melvin Belli Before the Reading of Mae West's Will," "John James Audubon Describes His Childhood to His Sons, Victor and Johnnie," "Joseph Mason, Audubon's Former Background Artist, Speaks to Their Mutual Friends on Loyalty," "Upon Taking Delivery of Audubon's First Published Bird Prints, Joseph Mason Sees, Then Shares with His Son, a Bitter Truth"

Mezzo Cammin: "Luz Bones," "Mae West to Her Longtime Lover Two Hours Before Her Attorney Arrives to Draft Her Will," "Nok Thai's Lullaby" (as "Nok Thai's Refrain to Chang and Eng") "The Last Known Words of Frederick Valentich from a Disc Discovered in a Field of Alfalfa," "A Farmer Reveals to His Best Mate the Details of His Sighting," "Guido Valentich to a Persistent Junior Reporter," "Alberta Valentich in Mourning for Her Son," "After Decades of Avoiding the Press, Rhonda Rushton Breaks Her Silence in a Televised Interview," "Stephen Roby, Former Air Traffic Controller and the Last Person to Talk with Frederick Valentich, Speaks on the Mystery of Valentich's Disappearance"

Nimrod: "Martin Luther, Plagued in His Retirement by Sickness, Appeals to His Wife," "Lord Katie, Three Days Before Christmas," "The Presbyterian Minister, Donald Cargill, to His Dead Wife on the Eve of His Execution," "Lucy Bakewell Audubon Takes Her Grandson on a Late-Night Walk to Find Her Husband," "John James Audubon's Late Refrains"

The Orchards: "Kat Ashley, First Lady of the Bedchamber, Reveals the Queen's Condition in a Letter to Her Beloved," "John Ashley, Master of the Queen's Jewels, in a Letter to His Still-Absent Wife"

River Styx: "The Anatomist, Dr. Antonio Maria Valsalva, Converses with His Young Bride Over Supper," "Annie C., Former Security Guard at Walmart, to Her Brother on Her Near-Death Experience"

Southwest Review: "Hans Christian Andersen Encloses His Miniature Likeness in a Letter to Jenny Lind," "Jenny Lind to Her Husband After He Discovers Her Cache of Letters from Hans Christian Andersen," "Riborg Voigt Bøving to Her Husband on His Objections to Hans Christian Andersen," "Hans Christian Andersen to a Confidant," "In a Letter to His Cousin, Banker Moritz Melchior Speaks of His Wife, Dorothea, and Her Devotion to Hans Christian Andersen," "Dorothea Melchior to Her Daughter on Andersen's Impact a Dozen Years After His Death"

Contents

PART III: AS PRESENT NOW AS EVER

Luz Bones

Prologue

Luz Bones

*—those bones comprising the coccyx, or tailbone, which according to legend
are the last to decay in the grave, thereby seemingly immortal*

Inside my father's, in life, staphylococcus
once colonized itself after its descent
from his heart, each rude metropolis
inhabiting a segment where pain, nascent,

then perverse, afflicted him for months.
And in my own, during both labors,
grew a torment that, remembered, stuns
me still. A Jewish tale says that the sabers

of Death neither rattle nor slay in the city
of Luz, all that God saved of Paradise
here, where dwellers live an eternity
unbound from the onus of sin. No device

is given the rest of us but to envision
the body's smallish afterlife: a core
of bones—five or less, brown or ashen,
ordered or erratic—within an earthen door.

I

PART I

Cast About as Vapor

Martin Luther, Plagued in His Retirement by Sickness, Appeals to His Wife

Wittenberg, Germany, 1536

I am confounded, Katie, that my heart,
aflutter like a candle flame, misbehaves
even here in our Eden of plenty, my cart
of beans, lettuces, and the cloven halves

of African watermelons our sons severed
in outright deviltry, too cumbrous for me
to push on this miry path. Am I embittered
by my ills? No, for the Lord God gave me

you. And you, my Lord Katie, shall salve
my heart tonight with your newest physic
of garlic, hawthorn, and onion. You saved
yourself years ago from your monastic

life by fleeing in a pickled herring barrel.
Do no less for me, love, in my peril.

Lord Katie, Three Days Before Christmas

Wittenberg, Germany, 1540

I have milked dear Biene and Liebling until
their udders are dry as Christmas stollen left
too long in the hearth oven, its raisin fill
akin to year-old rat dung. . . . Martin! Lift

the Yule tree onto the board so I may place
a linden crown and the last few Blaunderelly
apples on it . . . Paul, help your papa pace
himself, or there will be no salted pork belly

bacon in the skillet for you! And pen the dog
and the cock in the yard—for Heaven's sake,
child, latch the door! I hear, son, in Prague
a boy's shoes are filled with twigs if he takes

Jesus' name in vain. . . . Your tongue, Martin,
is huge, and speckled red. Let *me* say matins . . .

Kat Ashley, First Lady of the Bedchamber, Reveals the Queen's Condition in a Letter to Her Beloved

Hampton Court, England, November, 1562

Only to you, dear husband, do I dare
speak of her with such unsubtle frankness,
for you, John, above all others, are aware
that I tender her greater love than goodness
requires. When she arose early this morn
from her bath, she tried to conceal the scars
the pox has inflicted, and in her most forlorn
voice bemoaned her nose's recurring catarrh
and its flux. . . . I fear her spirit weakens
anew, and may soon succumb to melancholy.
She is no longer young, and what wakens
or sleeps within her seems but reckless folly.
She agrees to wed, but denies princes
from every able realm. Thus her favorite,
Dudley, finding her talk capricious, presses
her with increasing fervor. And still she flits
from yes to no like a wayward child. I bade
her to temper her sentiments with reason,
and dressed her, lacking Ann or Letty's aid.
Past noon it was before the task was done
and the last thimble-full of Dr. Huick's
orange-flower water cast about as vapor.
Now, her mood unleavened, she is fixed
on sleep tonight, though there is no leisure

for me, awake in my bed at the foot of hers.
Tomorrow, I shall offer her a goose confit
and candied plums to break her fast, a furz-
petal decoction, and much motherly heat.

John Ashley, Master of the Queen's Jewels, in a Letter to His Still-Absent Wife

The Jewel House, London, England, May, 1563

Sweet heart, I am afflicted here, though not
from ills occasioned by plague. I am fraught
by lack of any intercourse with you. How doth
our noble Bess deprive us from plying our troth
without a whit of conscience? . . . Ah, I hear it,
that familiar plea you ofttimes make for grit
in the face of duty, so without ado I surrender
to your wishes. A sound kiss you will tender
me, lady, when next we meet. . . . On this eve
at my desk, I curtail with your implied leave
an already much pared-down correspondence,
for I must check the stacks of silver plate once
more, then dispatch strands of Bess's pearls
for the Swedish ambassador's fête. Her furled
coils of Indian rubies, of diamonds, amethysts,
and the gold upon which they glitter and twist,
I would enlace you with, love, if I but dared.
Such is the daftness I indulge since she pried
us apart! Still, in my leisure, I have again begun
to study the patterns I perceive in a horse's run
when at its fullest gallop, though my investigation
pales when I think of you. Our Queen and nation
we will serve first—but O, dear Kat, dear wife,
how I long for the pleasures of a homelier life.

The Presbyterian Minister, Donald Cargill, to His Dead Wife on the Eve of His Execution

Edinburgh, Scotland, 26 July, 1681

Ah, sweet Margaret, how Sirius, our Dog Star,
visible, nay ghostly, through this leaded pane,
assuages my ache tonight. Think how far,
love, its light reigns. I shall not abstain

from speaking here of my death, or its ambit.
The King's Privy Council has found me guilty
of treason, and early on the morrow a gibbet,
arisen at the mercat cross, will claim me.

But first, to the throng, I shall repeat my plea
that no man has leave to dictate God's design.
Then, Margaret, at last my soul may flee
this earthly life, and will, like a lantern

at dusk, or Canis Major, now vaporous blue,
limn the light of heaven as I rejoin you.

The Rev. Donald Cargill's Brother, James, on Following a Merchant's Path

Glasgow, Scotland, 1682

I am not now, nor ever was, my brother's
keeper, and furthermore, the threat of Hell's
enduring fire, or the mayhem of his martyr's
end, hath for me no glory. Glasgow's bells,

in truth, doth merely call me to the haunt
of my living, bins of woolens and leathers
and homely trinkets beneath a leaky vault
of wattle and thatch beyond old Blackfriars

Church. . . . I earn there only coin enough
to sup each evening, and to nurse my ailing
wife and daughter. *They* are my own rough
religion, my safest refuge, my highest calling.

What need have I of any other, for they
offer me salvation. It is to them I pray.

The Anatomist, Dr. Antonio Maria Valsalva, Converses with His Young Bride Over Supper

Bologna, Italy, 1709

My initial foray into human terrain
was spawned, Elena, by my father's ear
out of which quite often flowed a strain
of viscous pus-filled fluid. Yes, my dear,

of course I tasted it, for I fathomed
even then that physicians should use every
sense in their diagnostics. Yet imagine
the sour tingling on my tongue no slurry

of oak bark blunted until the day grew
late. . . . Yes, yes, I see. . . . You now aim
to prevent my testing any cadaver's glue
if I wish to kiss you? How shall I claim

cures for the living with such a constriction?
Are you ill, wife?—or having a tantrum?

Elena to Her Second Husband, Niccolo,
on the Failings of Her First Husband

Rome, Italy, 1725

Though I was there but once, the air inside
his filthy, ill-lit surgery was malignant,
the posies in my bodice lame as walleyed
bowmen against a foe. Was I indignant,

love, at the iron odor of blood he wore
that day upon his cuffs, rusty as cook's
befouled pots? Need you ask? As sorely
as I ofttimes recall his face and bookish

blather, 'twas the day-old herring stench
embedded in the furring on his tongue
that I remember best. A lover wrenches
a whit of sugar off the cone with a tug

persuasive and delicate. Not my Antonio.
Croaker or no, he was all braggadocio.

Lucy Bakewell Announces Her Imminent
Marriage to John James Audubon in a Letter
to Her Kinswoman, Miss Gifford

Fatland Ford, near Valley Forge, Pennsylvania, 2 April, 1808

At the risk of unseemliness, I freely admit,
dear cousin, that my intended is, in his prime,
the most amply-favored of men. Tall, athletic,
and handsome, his face eloquent as a mime's,
he courted me chastely for three long years
until our fathers, initially against our union,
at last, in March, agreed to it. My sisters' tears
will, no doubt, drown our vows, to be spoken
Tuesday next, here at Fatland Ford in the parlor.
I shall be saddened to leave my siblings—since
Mama's death, I have acted more their mother
than sister—yet, as you know, love convinces
one to undertake every sort of misery. John
James and I will depart on the eighth of April
by coach, carried first to Philadelphia, then on
to Pittsburgh, where, he warns me, the peril
of a water passage to Kentucky awaits us.
I am not disturbed by his talk. I am, instead,
stirred by the vision we share: a conscious
life of the body, alert, supple, happily led
by its own desires, and a life of the mind
in every aspect its equal, even in Louisville
where John James, as half-owner, will mind

a general store while l teach *mademoiselles*
the feminine arts. In our free time we hope
to make music, me at my pianoforte, and he
at his fiddle — assuming they survive the trip.
And, as always, he will hunt the dowdy she
and bright he of birds. But, enough chatter.
l am off to roll the hall rug, dust the chandelier,
and chop a mountain of figs for the cake batter.
How l wish, dear girl, that you were here!

John James Audubon Describes His Childhood to His Sons, Victor and Johnnie

Henderson, Kentucky, Summer, 1819

In Saint-Domingue there was sun and sun
and the incessant chatter of sugar stalks
just beyond the verandah's view. Crimson
the sun set and crimson it rose while talk

burbled from Martine's kitchen like Latin
from Fr. Giles's tongue during daily mass
in the plantation chapel, his silver paten
mirroring his black hand as he passed

a host into each gaping mouth. Outside
the doors was a greensward and a border
of pines darkening a ridgeline, a wild divide
where once, I am convinced, I heard ardor

wax in a Vervain Hummingbird's delirium
of song. Though I was but six, I remember
well the whirring machinelike thrum
of his wings as he flew by, the somber

gray of his throat and chest. A sly Puritan
he was, with only a glint of metallic green
visible, then fugitive, a hue whose origin
is light and the bird's own preen-oil sheen.

Barely larger than a hawkmoth, a Vervain
is often taken at a blossom's end for a Bee
Hummingbird, which is smaller yet. I claim,
in truth, to have drawn one of each, and see

no good cause to kill another. When Father
returned to his villa in Nantes, France with us,
his bastard son and daughter, our stepmother
kissed us both at the door and pronounced us

home at last. We bless her, and her exemplary
virtue still—Anne Moynet, of the ardent
heart and barren womb, whose *l'orangerie*
in winter and garden in summer were parent

to the two most credulous of the villa's naif
dwellers: Rosie and I, afoot among the furred
and the winged, each mouse and bird a waif
whose name we printed in a book of words.

Joseph Mason, Audubon's Former Background Artist, Speaks to Their Mutual Friends on Loyalty

Philadelphia, Pennsylvania, Spring, 1832

Some prefer to label him a braggart
for calling himself *the* American Woodsman
while visiting London. And perhaps his heart
and his ego *were* inflated by women

fawning over his long hair and homey
fur-trimmed buckskin, or by the daily rags
that reported his gaze as *direct, intensely
wild*, and *dark as Satan's*. He crabs

now about the folly of that last bit,
though I quite suspect, boys, that flattered
by its reference to power, he secretly likes it.
Even dear Lucy, bless her soul, battered

by life with or without him, continues
to describe him as a *genius*, and *charismatic*
and who are we to dispute her? Our sinews,
muscles, minds, our local and domestic

lives, shall never rise to John James's
level of drama in excellence. I've seen him
lure birds with seeds and silence, dazed
at how quickly he rose and shot them

with his fine-pellet gun. His subscribers
ask him how he transfuses the breath of life
into such creatures. I can tell them: he scribes
a board with a grid, and before the bright

colors of the bird's wings dull, pins
its body to the wood in an approximation
of flight or stance, after which he outlines
on a corresponding graph its simulation.

He has a gift that will not be outdone
and he will make a fortune—mark my words—
thus we, as his friends, must seek to caution
him against overweening pride. In thirds

his heart is divided—by birds, by Lucy,
by his sons—and though he merits our affection
whether woodsman or artist, stable or swoony,
he may yet have need of our correction.

Upon Taking Delivery of Audubon's First Published
Bird Prints, Joseph Mason Sees, Then Shares with His
Son, a Bitter Truth

Philadelphia, Pennsylvania, January, 1835

I was but thirteen—clearly more boy than man
despite the confidence I affected—when Audubon
and I left for New Orleans to implement his plan
of recording undocumented birds, all drawn

to scale, while I, sketching beside him, rendered
their usual haunts: Blue Yellow-Backed Warblers
on a Coppery Iris, Painted Finches on a tender
Chickasaw Plum, a lone male Thrush atwitter

on an Indian Turnip. Come sunset, we slept
where we fell, exhausted, into beds of thigh-high
prairie grass or the piney earth beyond, kept
until birdsong woke us and a new day's supply

of specimens required our attention: wire
inserted into their wings, dousings in clear water
to deepen their colors, and later, of course, fire
to cook them over. . . . Even acts of slaughter,

boy, should occasion no waste. Yes, I prized
that life, for in it I found not merely my calling
but a man whose heart pumped the same blood.
Yet, how misplaced my trust, and how galling

his betrayal. Look at these prints. Do you see
anywhere at all, in any corner, *J. Mason*?
Here, and here, and here, this flora, these bees,
are mine in stroke after stroke, line after line!

Audubon denies, and falsifies, to fatten his ego.
His famed night in a cabin with Daniel Boone
on the edge of the wilderness is simply a blow-
hard's story, as is the tale of his father's spoon-

fed wealth. Why write, or call upon, or trace
him, or seek to cross paths with any of his kin?
Let us erase him with silence, just as he erased
my name from these works again and again.

Lucy Bakewell Audubon Takes Her Grandson on a Late-Night Walk to Find Her Husband

Minniesland, Manhattan, July, 1848

There has not been, nor shall not be
birdsong as beguiling as John James
mocking a mocker in our chokecherry

tree. Most birds, boy, both tame
and wild, are drawn to him as if by
magic, though I spy well his game.

His mind may ail but he is handy
still at palming seeds from his pocket.
Mockers thrive on weed seeds, Willie,

as you do on potatoes. Such thickets
as these are habitations for all sorts
of fliers—chats, thrashers, kinglets,

crows—yet only a mocker will resort
to song beneath the moon's whey-
faced light. What kind of true report

shall we make for John James's sake,
child, when he asks why we are out?
Yes, of course, what's apt: to take

him an oil lantern with nary a pout
at his absence again from the supper
table—his two most fervently devout

followers up and about to buffer
him, at least for one brief hour, from
his own befuddlement. Let us suffer

his load of midnight hubris and shun
nothing he will ask us to hear or see:
bird on the wing, the mocker's tune

neat and naive, a quixotic spree
of mimicry until he alights, perfectly
pat and plumb, on John James's knee.

John James Audubon's Late Refrains

Minniesland, Manhattan, November, 1850

1
If I sleep now, Lucy, even for a moment,
four-winged birds with pointed heads appear,

small and quick as bees, their song a lament.
If I sleep now, Lucy, even for a moment,

Satan himself births more in a raw foment
of color, each one puce, beautiful, but queer.

If I sleep now, Lucy, even for a moment,
four-winged birds with pointed heads appear.

2
I will not eat the potato—whether cooked
or raw. You are a fool if you think I shall.

A dead tabby pissed on it twice, the spook.
I will not eat the potato, whether cooked,

mashed, fried, or scalloped, even if yoked
to our table, wife, like an ox to his plow.

I will not eat the potato—whether cooked
or raw. You are a fool if you think I shall.

3

Never shoot ravens, Willie, for they return
as heralds of the dead to infest these oaks

in which they squall and thrash and preen.
Never shoot ravens, Willie, for they return

charred as chimney soot. Each still burns
with spite, boy, and every caw provokes.

Never shoot ravens, Willie, for they return
as heralds of the dead to infest these oaks.

4

What a pretty little parrot you are, Lynette.
Here, have a bite of my potato, *ma cherie* . . .

Ah, I see you are still quite the coquette.
What a pretty little parrot you are, Lynette,

on my arm in the wildwood where moonset
advances. Today, the very sky is your aerie.

What a pretty little parrot you are, Lynette.
Here, have a bite of my potato, *ma cherie*.

PART II

The Siamese Twins Narratives

*Which would you prefer, that I . . . sever the flesh
that connects you or cut off your heads? One will
produce just about the same results as the other.*

—Chang and Eng Bunker's physician,
after being asked to separate them following
an argument that had nearly come to blows

Nok Thai's Lullaby

Province of Samut Songkhram, Siam, 1811

You are two, two you are,
my right, my left, my near, my far,

before whom every village mother
averts her eyes, and every father

calls upon Buddha. You are two,
two you are, my boy babes new

as herons in the spring-fed swell
of the Mae Klong, where men tell

tales of you first spun by your bàba,
heads awry, eyes round as casabas

or coconuts. You are two, two
you are, a mewling clamor askew

in the air, demanding milk
and the heated skin of saffron silk

that lines my robe, which you savor
beyond reason. O, may you favor

the little balm of sleep till dawn
under our weave of mango fronds.

You are two, two you are,
my right, my left, my near, my far.

Nok Thai in Mourning for Her Husband

Province of Samut Songkhram, Siam

August, 1819

After midday, when rains thrum on the thatch,
my children dream in their hammocks. It is then
that he comes only to me, home from the catch
and showered clean in the river's fall, his thin

arms filled with Hidden Lilies and Jasmine buds
whose colors and scents he scatters over the dirt
floor, or places in the baskets suspended above
our heads. He is silent, even with his parrot, Preet,

who ails in his absence and also does not speak.
Always, in these visitations, he is but a shadow
whom I can neither hold nor press my cheek
against. Afterwards, in the tears that follow,

I taste the brine of his first love—the sea
that both fed him, and took him from me.

October, 1820

Chang and Eng, old enough now, go about
their father's work. The village mothers watch
them scuttle up and down our roof while bound
together by rope as they repair the thatch.

The mothers' eyes are slits from which disgust
and anger glitter. How have they not yet seen
that fear, not my boys, is the monster that thrusts
itself into our midst? Why have they not gleaned

relief from the Buddha, whose heart teaches us
courage even in the full unfolding of our fear?
The boys are nine, and strong, and still trust
what I ask them to believe. Yet they near

an age when Bangkok's spoils will lure them.
How shall I keep them safe from peril then?

Nok Thai on the Thought of New Lives for Herself and Her Children

Province of Samut Songkhram, Siam, April, 1825

Praise to the Buddha, who today delivered us
favor in the presence of a man named Hunter
who comes to us from the highland of Scots.

Inside my humble doorway, my daughter, such
a curious monkey, gazed wide-eyed as a tarsier
at his clothes, which clung to his body much

as a liana vine clings to a tree. He claimed
to bring us happiness, then gave me a basket
of whole cloth and Malee a clever game

called Fox and Geese. To Chang and Eng,
whom he had seen swimming in the river,
he told strange tales of cities blossoming

across the green bounds of the seven seas.
He would, he said, pay me to exhibit them
there, and from his profits pay them fees.

Four days after I birthed them, King Chim,
declaring them a monster, vowed to slay them.
A monk confessed later that what stayed him

was the sacred breath of a raven whispering
no in his ear. Now, his successor, Nangklao,
sits upon his father's throne, warning

of the world beyond and its great hungers.
If my boys go, will they thrive? And who
will sell my duck eggs in Bangkok? Hunter

is with them now in the mangos, and they,
little mynahs, repeat his words. I have killed
an old hen and prepared curry with bay

and cilantro for their supper, yet still they
linger. If the King approves, I will let them
go, though my heart bid them stay.

Captain Abel Coffin on How He and His Partner,
Robert Hunter, Have Managed the Twins on Tour

Boston, Massachusetts, August, 1829

Aye, good boys they was, good boys both,
till six months past when their dispositions
soured. No fool she, their mother, loathe
to play the harpy with us on our disruptions

of her payments, bleated instead to Eng.
The woman was five hundred dollars richer
than she had ever been after surrendering
her sons to our promotion, yet her choler

had risen over Rob's failure to send off
the twenty-five hundred still promised her.
"Ah, it's debtor's prison for us," Rob scoffed
as we floated, coached, or rode, ushering

the twins through America's wallets. Now,
a short stroll off the Common up in Boylston
Hall, "The Siamese Double Boys" have plowed
much of Boston's elite. . . . They are beacons

at the box office with takes beyond our ken.
It's a fine enterprise we've found, the shows
fresh and unscripted. The audience, shaken
when the boys first appear, soon undergoes

a transformation, its stunned silence evolving
into a murmurous hum of awe and approval,
the boys' tricks and native dignity dissolving
even the skeptics' reserve. Prior to our arrival

in New England, Chang and Eng had conquered
English, and now sail just as easily through
French and Italian, both of which will spur
our effect in Europe. Time, it seems, hews

to a heightened pace, and the twins, faster
than we can imagine, will reach their majority.
Thus, Rob and I calculate we must make haste
to book the venues in Paris soon, and heavily.

I, Chang-Eng

Liverpool Road Railway Station, Manchester, England, 12 March, 1832

The people come in droves to see us run
and jump and tumble in our one on one

cohesion over the burnished gaslit boards
of theaters in Paris, Prague, Omsk, and Linz,

their mouths little O's of surprise, or distaste,
or empathy, as we entertain them, first in haste,

then standing still for their onerous inspections.
Worse yet are the surgeons' mock dissections

conducted onstage in city after city as they
poke and prod and declare us true as day,

the glint of avarice in their eyes. Two months
from now we come of age and out from under

Hunter and Coffin's thumbs, and shall accede
only to one another's wishes. Not greed,

but ambition shall enliven us as we embark
again for America and its venues. In Newark,

New York, and Boston, we will measure men
whose purported skill may, at long last, lend

itself to our separation. If they do not succeed,
then Buddha wishes it so. No earthly creed

we know can then prevent us from seeking lives
in the homely heat of our own hearth and wives.

Nancy Yates on Her Daughters' Upcoming Double Nuptials

Wilkesboro, North Carolina, 10 April, 1843

Three days hence our Addie will claim her heart's
desire, Chang Bunker, despite my cautions
and her father's concerns, while Sally departs
maidenhood to be joined to Eng. The emotions

the boys try to hide I sense—a glorysome
bliss in Chang, and a slow chary hopefulness
in Eng that one day, perhaps, Sally will come
to feel for him more intensely. Needfulness

has its place in marriage, and Sally's soul
is sweet and eminently pliable, unlike Addie's
which knows only its own wants. What role
Grace will play, however, other than mammy

to the children, will be up to Grace herself. She
is our gift to our daughters in their new lives,
and though we give her to them happily,
we shall miss her sorely. . . . Less than five

months ago, the boys left for Philadelphia
in great secrecy, having arranged to be separated.
They were found at the door of the surgical arena
by the girls, who wept and wailed and berated

them, and by Grace, who promptly bullied them
into their clothes and home again. Their actions—
understandable, and foolishly selfless—stemmed,
no doubt, from distress about the transactions

of the marital bed, a thought I shall not plow. . . .
The wedding breakfast following the early ceremony
will be here in our parlor, large enough now
thanks to those "unable" to attend. Such acrimony

towards the Bunkers overrides both reason
and decorum. Nevertheless, we will celebrate
with wine and toasts aplenty to the fruitful season
of our daughters' unions with the boys they liberate.

I, Chang-Eng

The Bunker Farm, Surry County, North Carolina, August, 1864

We are two, two we are,
no longer travelers near and far,

North Carolina our chosen nation,
a thousand acres our plantation

along Stewarts Creek on either side.
There, we and our wives abide

close by White Plains and Mt. Airy
in two houses—one for Addie,

one for Sally—where we oversee
in bedsteads large enough for three

the war the South wages. Out there
just shy of the Potomac somewhere

our sons ride with the other boys
of the Thirty-Seventh Virginia Calvary

under Gen. McCausland's command.
May it please the Buddha to remand

them home to us and their mothers alive.
Our slaves, nattering like bees in hives

this evening, read in the raw entrails
of a chicken that the war's travails

soon will end. In what caprice
then descends we want no piece.

We are two, two we are,
no longer travelers near and far,

North Carolina our chosen nation,
a thousand acres our plantation.

Aunt Grace Yates on the Brink of Change

The Bunker Farm, Surry County, North Carolina, April, 1865

It be going on twelve years I done traveled
betwixt Miz Sally's and Miz Addie's houses
till my bones is tired and my brains addled.
Yes'um, yes'um, I say, but up then rouses

in me a queerness, like a faint coming crude,
or a spell of ire. I is who held and raised them
girls up from diapers to dolls to motherhood,
but they done act like Satan hisself hails from

the other. There be no such tripe for the twins
I done cotton to now. . . . Them boys is sweet,
or not, when they talk, but know they be kin
of the nighest kind. I fixes my best buckwheat

cakes for those two more than twice a week,
though Eng hankers less than Chang. I says
to Eng, *you ain't got a fire like your peaked
brother*. They is the most tolerable massas

I ever did see. . . . They be talking long now,
with Miz Sally and Miz Addie, 'bout letting
us darkies go since the War sours, but vow
I will stay. Chang says, *Grace, I am betting*

you'd take wages without batting an eye,
but I just grins and keeps right on cleaning.
This be home, wage or not. The land's awry,
but praise God, I is here till Hell is greening.

Dr. James Calloway, to His Protégé,
on His History with the Bunker Brothers

Wilkesboro, North Carolina, August, 1874

I first met them at Peale's New York Museum
in the mid-1830's, and must admit
I was surprised at their finely-honed erudition

gained not from the pages of books, but from life
itself. They were quick as any two men
I've known, and many were the fools rife

with arrogance who deduced that fact too late.
That very first night, in their dressing room
under the stage, I felt an affection for them both,

though they were, indeed, quite different, Eng's
temper steady as this metronome, while
Chang's blew hot, then hotter, till it sprang,

it seemed, straight from the forge of Hell. Still, they
each displayed a singular purity of feeling
for those who'd been dispossessed, and portrayed

themselves—despite having gained the entire world—
among that number. I had what they wanted:
a home, and property enough to live undisturbed.

After two days in their company, I invited them
to Wilkesboro, extolling it and our county's
splendors. When they at last arrived they came

for good. For thirty years I hitched up my bays
and drove out to doctor them, their wives,
their broods and slaves, our friendship paving

the way. Yet, in the end, I could not save them
from each other, in life or in the grave,
just as I cannot save myself from my own

decay. Such a little jig we do, John, truly,
for Death stalks us all forever and
a day. Loyalty is our only lasting beauty.

Sally Bunker Looks Back on Her Marriage

Mt. Airy, North Carolina, Summer, 1875

It seemed to me, at least when it was green,
a union of convenience, rather than ardor,
and indeed it was Addie—having never been
denied—who stoked the twins' marriage fever

and the proceedings from end to end. Only
after our third child's birth did Eng and I
grow close enough to see our own synchrony,
while Addie and Chang, bickerers both, vivified

each other from the first. The children came
forthwith—eleven for me, ten for Addie—
and most survived infancy. If I felt shame,
it was not for myself, my sister, or our progeny,

but for the parochial minds of men who said
the devil's work took place in our marital beds.

Addie Bunker on Her Sister and
Their Conjoined and Separate Lives

Mt. Airy, North Carolina, 14 March, 1892

We both began to fatten in our middle
years, no chores or cares or forced subsistence
lessening our girth. Now, though often idle,
Sally wastes away, her body and countenance

ever more skeletal. Yes, we skirmished . . .
we surely did . . . for access to our husbands
and attention for our children, for land,
chattels, goods. But if our wounds were wounds

of want, they were also those of necessity
for which neither of us need speak with regret.
Once, we were the fairest belles in Surry
County, raised up to marry the finest of gents,

yet it was I who played the cleverest game
by securing us each both love *and* fame.

Robert Bunker Describes the Circumstances of His Father's Death

Mt. Airy, North Carolina, June, 1948

Though I was but eleven I remember well
that awful morn when Pa, in a voice chafed
with pain, tremulous and breathy, compelled
me to quickly light a taper and make haste

to his room just down the hall. And when
I entered it was clear, even in the flickering
light, even to me, that Uncle Chang was gone.
My father's face was rigid, clouds escaping

from his mouth in the wintry air. Then Ma
entered the room and all turned to chaos—
her cries, her tears, her hands on Pa's jaw,
neck, arms, back and legs, the utter pathos

of her efforts to warm his flesh with hers.
As she worked, she began at last to direct
us, sending my older brother and Old Irv
to fetch the doctor, and my sister to collect

hot water, rags, and opium. I wanted Ma
to send *me* out of that room, into the dark
where I could breathe again. It was Pa's
terror filling him like rain fills a hoofmark

in mud that scared me, for I hadn't gathered
yet that his life, too, was compromised. . . .
Three hours after Chang passed, my father
followed him. Some since have theorized

that he literally died of fright, including
his own doctor, who arrived much too late.
But I believe Pa could not imagine living
any life in which Chang did not dominate.

These are my father's last words whole:
Then I am going, followed three hours later
by *May the Lord have mercy upon my soul*.
I pray the good Lord granted his desire.

PART III

As Present Now as Ever

Hans Christian Andersen Encloses His Miniature Likeness in a Letter to Jenny Lind

Copenhagen, Denmark, January, 1845

I must confess, my secret friend, that I
still suffer like a maiden at my bleak,
too-patent flaws: these pale, myopic eyes,
this pockmarked cheek and Himalayan beak

my looking glass mirrors its fool after.
Yet I have faith that your regard for me
shall not be lessened by my youthful limner's
veracity, which I pray only serves, Jenny,

to remind you of your most emphatic fan.
What joy I have taken in your conquest
of Berlin in Bellini's *Norma*! No woman
alive inspires me more than you to persist

in writing my latest tales. You guide my hand
and spirit, and therefore I remain, your Hans.

Jenny Lind to Her Husband After He Discovers Her Cache of Letters from Hans Christian Andersen

Dresden, Germany, June, 1852

If you have read them, Otto, you must accept
they merely speak of friendship in the way
a man like Hans—odd, inelegant, bereft
of adoration—might. He does not stray

into hyperbole, since from his pen or mouth
such falseness would be obvious. If beauty
has its persuasion, plainness has its clout
in purpose. Think of Hans as I do, his duty

to his art bringing time and again to fruition
his clever tales, though he has no consort
to recite the genius of his compositions.
We would do well to wish him the port

of a lenient lover, her warmth, her sighs,
as he lies blessedly spent between her thighs.

Riborg Voigt Bøving to Her Husband on His Objections to Hans Christian Andersen

Copenhagen, Denmark, Winter, 1855

You have no reason, Poul, for your aversion.
Why not take him in hand, that hapless man,
as you might take a starving dog or orphan
child? Hans's life, unlike your own, began

in privation, his father a cobbler, his mother
a sot. Too young he was put to work drying
tobacco in a factory, until six of the other
boys pulled his britches down, each vying

for proof that he was a girl. His nose, Poul,
is long, his eyes too small and closely-set,
and when he walks he lopes, a rustic fool,
some say, of nervy habits. Nevertheless,

he is a polished writer and clever wit,
and I shall buy his books as I see fit.

Hans Christian Andersen to a Confidant

Paris, France, 1867

Of course, I have some understanding of
a courtesan's life since my own half-sister,
Karen Marie, once plied the profit thereof
in lieu of honest earnings. And bestirred,

does any man not freely indulge a facile
lapse from his lonely, masturbatory bed?
In truth, I myself have done so, dazzled
by Mlle. Monique's green wit in the Red

Bordello in Pigalle—twenty francs I gave
for her cheeky intercourse—yet she rivals
neither my Jenny's splendor, nor my brave
and pious Riborg's pity. Though my revels

revolve around them—and Karl and Ervin—
I am destined to leave this life a virgin.

In a Letter to His Cousin, Banker Moritz Melchior Speaks of His Wife, Dorothea, and Her Devotion to Hans Christian Andersen

Rolighed House, near Copenhagen, 6 August, 1875

You do recall, Iris, that Andersen was one
of Ditte's bosom friends, as well as mine,
and therefore it was to her, and to her alone,
that he proclaimed his heart's labyrinthine

needs. Abed for weeks in our best chamber,
Andersen merely had to utter Ditte's name,
and she, happy nurse, would swiftly clamber
up the staircase with cloth and pail, game

to the last. Thus when death finally came for
him, it was dear Ditte who, always adroit,
unfastened from his neck the pouch he wore
and read the letter inside by Riborg Voigt,

composed so long ago. Selfless love, Iris,
is rare, and rarer still if it survives us.

Dorothea Melchior to Her Daughter on Andersen's Impact a Dozen Years After His Death

Rolighed House, near Copenhagen, Summer, 1887

Sometimes I find myself searching mail
from London or Berne for *Mrs. D. Melchior*
in Andersen's plain hand, as though he prevails
still. Of course, Louise, mawkishness calls for

this very sort of fancy, though I avow
that Andersen is as present now as he ever was.
Have you not noticed that men, reading aloud
his *Little Match Girl* to their children, pause

to wipe their own eyes and noses, or that
women like us, bereft of beauty, have seen
ourselves in his *Ugly Duckling*? Yes, chitchat
this well may be, but even before his spleen

gave out, a giant sculpture of him by Saabye
was underway, a true likeness, but stately.

Mae West to Her Longtime Lover Two Hours Before Her Attorney Arrives to Draft Her Will

The Ravenswood, Los Angeles, California, 1966

Sweet Paulie, sweet baby boy, treat me good
and warm my cup of steak juice. It's moronic
to sip it chilled. . . . Of course I've taken food
today—some Beluga caviar—and my colonic,
as usual, at six. A pussyfoot, love, you're not,
but must you do each task as though it's triage
and you're Doc Laskey back from Hell? Put
the jar of Ponds right here. . . . I'll massage
my breasts myself. . . . Ah, juice is better, pet,
quite hot. Now go and fetch my soaking teeth
and the green silk number I wore in *Sextette*.
No, wait, I want the aqua Edith Head sheath
instead. I'm going to look like a zillion zillion
when I divvy up my forty million.

Paul Novak to Attorney Melvin Belli
Before the Reading of Mae West's Will

Los Angeles, California, February, 1981

I'm not here to argue with those who think
I stayed with her only for her money.
I can talk and talk, but they won't blink.
No, I've come to say she was a glory
out of which, I swear, a sort of light shone
onscreen and off. Take a look at her
at nearly forty in *I'm No Angel*. Anyone
can see why Cary Grant adored her,
as I did, for I swear I was put here on earth
to care for her, to calm, kiss, and cosset
her. So tell me, what old spleen gives birth
to this gossip that beneath her corset
were hermaphroditic organs? . . . Melvin,
you know she was every inch a woman.

H. L. Describes His Recent Near-Death Experience to the Newest Member of His Sex Addiction Therapy Group

Chicago, Illinois, October, 1975

Imagine fright created not by blood
but by the striped impression of a grate
burning up your backside, no tunnel, no flood
of light, no mother, father, friend, or mate
in sight. Your goose is cooked, you're DOA,
chum, and there's fire below. The dire plight
of skin on sear can force a man to pray,
recanting every traitorous carnal night
until a finger, poking through the mass
of smoke above, then a hand and forearm
so stout they must be God's, plucks your ass
back into life. You're bridled, pal, and charm's
a bygone jig, but you've been good and rooted
inside Him. It'll keep you clean, stupid.

H. L.'s Former Wife, Mary, on His Checkered History

Palos Hills, Illinois, November, 1976

His mama warned me when I married him
that Hank was like a big dumb dog who needed
stroking day and night. "And that's a shame,"
she said, "because he's apt to roam." Needling
was what his mama always did best, but sure
enough, she was right. Turns out he schmucked
around for years—his charm on steroids tour—
until I'd had my fill. . . . *It's clear I'm fucked,*
he said when he came to, up out of a coma
and back from Hell, *unless I change my views
on screwing.* Then, in a blink, his mama
swept in and whisked him away. What news
I have of him now is from his sister, Constance,
who swears he loves his new life of abstinence.

Annie C., Former Security Guard at Walmart, to Her Brother on Her Near-Death Experience

Detroit, Michigan, July, 1977

I chased them three pinchers out of the store
and had my hand on one's shoulder when
I plunked down on the curb, dead as a door-
nail. I ain't lying. Fifty-nine minutes, Len,
I was out of this old body while Doc here
shocked me sixteen times. He got zilch,
but I didn't mind since I was swigging pear
juice up on Granny Cole's big white porch
when our two dear aunties sashayed by like
movie stars they was so pretty. I trained
along behind them, all lamb-and-dove-like,
with not a single spiteful word in my brain.
I didn't want to come back! Granny Cole
made me. Now, I'm a bona fide miracle.

In Line at the Celestial Coffee & Dessert Buffet, Annie's Auntie Alice Chats Up Her Sister

Heaven, Time Indeterminate

Oh Lordy, Lordy, what a stubborn pup
our Annie remains, refusing to leave here
or mind her elders until Mama, puffed up
with God's officious grace, blew her hare-
brained spirit back into her earthly body.
Yet all the high jinks Mama hated I found
sublimely entertaining—Annie's gaudy,
clownish rictus of a grin and big eyes round
and bright as brand new pie tins telling us
that she'll be back. Sooner than later's fine
with me, for Heaven's dreary after the fuss—
yes, decaf, dearie—of dying's left behind,
ain't that so, sister? Winona, God dang!
You gonna hog that last cocoa meringue?

The Last Known Words of Frederick Valentich from a Disc Discovered in a Field of Alfalfa

Date of Recording, and of this Transcription, Indeterminate

Since my abduction, I have no trustworthy method
of fixing time, and so am forced to merely guess
at its passage. Often I dream I'm suspended

in the Cessna's cockpit as the huge phantasmic craft
attaches itself to the plane's roof with a zippering,
metallic rasp, and suddenly I'm higher aloft

than ever before in the starless bowl of darkness
above Bass Strait. . . . Or, perhaps it's no dream.
Perhaps I'm *living* it again, for I confess

that buried in the bowels of the craft I neither sleep,
digest, or defecate—nor envision any possible
future that folds me back inside the sweep

of a human embrace. Of you, Pop, if you hear this,
I ask forgiveness for fancying myself equipped
to fly beyond dusk, though I feel bliss

in imagining how you and Mama, Sis and Richie,
and even my darling Rhonda's friends, adore
my memory now. If I am dead, and bully

for me if I am, every fiend here was surely bred
to effect that end. They're masters of attrition—
opaque as shadows on a wall—who embed

their designs in my head. But you know the facts
by now: I'm no longer the Freddie you loved.
Still, overflying Melbourne tonight, I lack

nothing mortal in the pleasure I take at the city's
beauty. It's a whacked-out mesmerizing sheen
upon which not even God pours His pity.

A Farmer Reveals to His Best Mate
the Details of His Sighting

New South Wales, Australia, 25 October, 1978

C'mon, Archie! I wasn't pissed on a workday.
I was filling the Allis's radiator when *it*
cruised, like a bloody phantom, over the bay

of the barn. It was shiny, and big—at least
thirty meters wide, I swear—and silent
as a snake before it strikes. My gut's atwist

now just thinking about it, but if I don't tell,
I'll go crackers. . . . Yes, it was low!
Then it stopped, and hovered, and like a bell,

vibrated, while all the while a single-prop plane
was stuck to the underbelly of the thing,
bobbling like a cork in water as oil drained

from its engine. You think I'm telling a porky,
but I can prove what I say. Here, look
at the Allis's fender—these letters, VH-D

SJ, were painted on the plane's side! . . . Why
else would I deliberately scratch the Allis
up with a nail, mate?. . . This is bona fide

proof that Valentich was taken. . . . Of course,
I didn't *see* him . . . I *never* said he waved
at me. . . . Christ, you're such a horse's arse!

Guido Valentich to a Persistent Junior Reporter

Victoria, Australia, March, 1979

No one who knows my son has *ever* believed
he was running drugs or would have wanted
to disappear. If you think he's dirty, leave
now. I've had my fill of being confronted

by the likes of you sniffing around like dogs
for a new take on the story. . . . He said what?
Why would Freddy talk about his flight logs,
or anything else, with you? I don't give a whit

if you spoke to him for two hours, or a minute.
You don't know him. And why would I accept
he's dead when there's no solid proof?—bits
from the plane, say, or some obvious effects

from his body, or the body itself. . . . Yes,
those could offer closure. But in lieu of that,
I've got to think of him as absent, in a place
beyond my imagining that allows no clear-cut

means of escape. . . . Oh, he's brave, all right.
No one's braver . . . and if he lacks restraint
at times, well, show me someone who doesn't.
Don't you, Mr. Jones, since you're a bit wet

yet behind the ears? Freddie bends rules
as young men tend to do, always in a hurry
to grow up and away from their over-schooled
boyhoods and their fathers' sway. . . . Bury

him I may, but for now he's still my first-
born son, alive and aloft in an unknown route
above the earth—still Freddy, yet rebirthed
again and again in your endless eye of doubt.

Alberta Valentich in Mourning for Her Son

Victoria, Australia, Summer, 1979

1
In dreams Freddy comes to me unbidden,
his face still his own, yet utterly changed,

cryptic as a feral cat's, wide and wooden.
In dreams Freddy comes to me unbidden

and bereft of affection, as if his heart, riven
from mine, will forever remain estranged.

In dreams Freddy comes to me unbidden,
his face still his own, yet utterly changed.

2
I swear I saw him today, lounging against
a lamppost on Collins St. in Port Phillip,

eyeing diamond rings, small to immense.
I swear I saw him today, lounging against

the wall at Hare & Grace, his lips tensed
as he fixed his gaze on a diner's rarebit.

I swear I saw him today, lounging against
a lamppost on Collins St. in Port Phillip.

3

What is it that day after day Roscoe spies
eight feet up where wall and wall meet?

He thumps his tail and his slobber flies.
What is it that day after day Roscoe spies

for minutes on end, lifetimes for a spitz-
dachshund mix short on brains but sweet.

What is it that day after day Roscoe spies
eight feet up where wall and wall meet?

After Decades of Avoiding the Press, Rhonda Rushton Breaks Her Silence in a Televised Interview

Victoria UFO Australia Convention, Melbourne, 6 September, 2014

1
I'd planned to fly with Fred the very day
his plane went missing, but ended instead
staying another shift at the shop, my delay
occasioned by a held-up co-worker. Fred
knew the pull of both duty and the world's
disorder. He would've understood. The week
before, he'd taken me to dinner and twirled
a friendship ring onto my finger, cheekily
hinting at the diamond he'd put in lay-by.
All of this happened thirty-six years ago
when I was just sixteen and Fred twenty,
yet ever since, in every new cockcrow,
in every transition of twilight into night,
I bring him back from that long last flight.

2
Of course I loved him. His mother knows
I always have and always will. Why do you
suppose that she and Fred's father, Guido,
gave me this diamond ring less than two
months after Fred's disappearance? It was
a gesture to honor his intent, although it's
not the ring he chose. . . . No, *that* ring was

"lost," according to the jeweler, who lifted
it from lay-by to resell despite our receipt.
Life likes to jolt us, doesn't it? As for me,
I'm still drawn to men who are helpmeets
and respectful, who ask the best of the me
that I've become. . . . Yes, they do enthrall.
Yet Fred, alive or dead, outshines them all.

Stephen Roby, Former Air Traffic Controller
and the Last Person to Talk with Frederick Valentich,
Speaks on the Mystery of Valentich's Disappearance

Melbourne, Australia, 5 April, 2015

After nearly four decades
Freddy's voice is as familiar today
in my memory as it is in the audio
transcript of his call: its odd array

of wonder and panic overlaid by
his last-ditch attempt to conduct
himself in a calm, reasoned manner.
And of course, as usual, the DOT

was in error. Only NASA's voice
analysis program had it right: he was
not, they confirmed, *matter-of-fact*,
but was *genuinely stressed*. The cause,

I argue, was not the planet Venus,
nor Freddy himself lost upside down
in a graveyard spiral into the Strait,
but what he said he saw—a green

light bathing an amorphous craft
of cigar-like proportions that first flew
beneath him, then hovered above him.
This encounter, which happened due

south-east of Cape Marengo, was seen
and sworn to by witnesses on the ground
who'd pulled off the road to watch. . . .
That night, Freddy and I were bound

together as surely as I am bound
today to the last members of his family.
They're good, honest people. But only
Guido believed, as I do, that one day

Freddy will come home. Until then,
until the water gives him up, or the ether,
we'll continue to gather at his memorial
on the coast of Cape Otway each October.

Epilogue

To My Parents in the Hereafter

1

Does your mother, Estella, come to you,
Father, toting biscuits and sausage gravy?

Are you six and ten at once, cast in blue?
Does your mother, Estella, come to you

trailing your siblings, that rowdy crew—
or are you twelve, tough, nobody's baby?

Does your mother, Estella, come to you,
Father, toting biscuits and sausage gravy?

2

Are you loved there, Mother, as you were
here? Is your diadem floral, or obsidian?

Who buys you Snickers, who buys you fur?
Are you loved there, Mother, as you were

here? In the cosmic wind is your line a blur
of angel down, or Father's sodden woolens?

Are you loved there, Mother, as you were
here? Is your diadem floral, or obsidian?

3
Where will I find you, or will you find me
abroad in Zion? Will I feel my remaking?

Is joy synchronous in the astral sea?
Where will I find you, or will you find me?

Are souls distinguishable, are they free,
or bound each to each in an infinite waking?

Where will I find you, or will you find me
abroad in Zion? Will I feel my remaking?

Books from Etruscan Press

Zarathustra Must Die | Dorian Alexander
The Disappearance of Seth | Kazim Ali
Drift Ice | Jennifer Atkinson
Crow Man | Tom Bailey
Coronology | Claire Bateman
What We Ask of Flesh | Remica L. Bingham
The Greatest Jewish-American Lover in Hungarian History | Michael Blumenthal
No Hurry | Michael Blumenthal
Choir of the Wells | Bruce Bond
Cinder | Bruce Bond
The Other Sky | Bruce Bond and Aron Wiesenfeld
Peal | Bruce Bond
Poems and Their Making: A Conversation | Moderated by Philip Brady
Crave: Sojourn of a Hungry Soul | Laurie Jean Cannady
Toucans in the Arctic | Scott Coffel
Body of a Dancer | Renée E. D'Aoust
Scything Grace | Sean Thomas Dougherty
Surrendering Oz: A Life in Essays | Bonnie Friedman
Nahoonkara | Peter Grandbois
The Candle: Poems of Our 20th Century Holocausts | William Heyen
Confessions of Doc Williams & Other Poems | William Heyen
The Football Corporations | William Heyen
A Poetics of Hiroshima | William Heyen
Shoah Train | William Heyen
September 11, 2001, American Writers Respond | Edited by William Heyen
American Anger: An Evidentiary | H. L. Hix
As Easy As Lying | H. L. Hix
As Much As, If Not More Than | H. L. Hix
Chromatic | H. L. Hix
First Fire, Then Birds | H. L. Hix
God Bless | H. L. Hix
I'm Here to Learn to Dream in Your Language | H. L. Hix
Incident Light | H. L. Hix
Legible Heavens | H. L. Hix
Lines of Inquiry | H. L. Hix

Etruscan Press Is Proud of Support Received From

Wilkes University

Youngstown State University

The Raymond John Wean Foundation

The Ohio Arts Council

The Stephen & Jeryl Oristaglio Foundation

The Nathalie & James Andrews Foundation

The National Endowment for the Arts

The Ruth H. Beecher Foundation

The Bates-Manzano Fund

The New Mexico Community Foundation

Drs. Barbara Brothers & Gratia Murphy Foundation

The Rayen Foundation

The Pella Corporation

Founded in 2001 with a generous grant from the Oristaglio Foundation, Etruscan Press is a nonprofit cooperative of poets and writers working to produce and promote books that nurture the dialogue among genres, achieve a distinctive voice, and reshape the literary and cultural histories of which we are a part.

etruscan press
www.etruscanpress.org

Etruscan Press books may be ordered from

Consortium Book Sales and Distribution
800.283.3572
www.cbsd.com

Etruscan Press is a 501(c)(3) nonprofit organization.
Contributions to Etruscan Press are tax deductible
as allowed under applicable law.
For more information, a prospectus,
or to order one of our titles,
contact us at books@etruscanpress.org.